D1082948

My Friend
ERNEST HEMINGWAY

My Friend
ERNEST HEMINGWAY

An Affectionate Reminiscence

By William Seward

South Brunswick and New York: A. S. Barnes and Co.
London: Thomas Yoseloff Ltd

A. S. Barnes and Co., Inc.
Cranbury, New Jersey

Thomas Yoseloff Ltd
108 New Bond Street
London W1Y OQX, England

SBN 498-07336-X

Printed in the United States of America

To
Virginia

Preface

Perhaps it will seem ironic to many readers that a college professor of English has written reminiscences of a friendship with Ernest Hemingway, who in general had a very low opinion of academic and literary people. Nevertheless, I have the happy distinction of being an exception, a professional teacher with whom he was friendly. A few impressions from this relationship, it seems to me, are now in order.

According to an eminent critic, Hemingway, before he was cold in his grave, suffered jealous and sneering attacks by piddling little writers unworthy to lick his boots. My hope is to help make at least a small start toward setting the record straight: to counteract some of the biographers and critics who have written out of envy and in very bad taste as well as those who have indulged in questionable details that read more like sensational gossip than fact.

The man I knew was an adventurer and a compulsive reader, a sportsman and a husband and father, an athlete and a businessman. But most of all he was an artist with well-nigh unlimited interests and talents. Always, the marvelous side of Ernest's intellection is what came through to me most and I hope it is what will come through to the reader. After all, when he was not writing, he felt he was wasting his life.

Although I did not see much of Ernest Hemingway personally, we maintained a twenty-year, informal correspondence, which in some ways can be more revealing than constant in-the-flesh association, since letters are one of the friendliest forms of intercourse. Ernest, himself, has remarked that you write a friend and have much the same contact as though you were together: you exchange letters and it is almost as good as talking. Yet he discouraged the publication of his letters, so I have not reproduced them verbatim but instead have attempted to paraphrase sections that are pertinent to the purposes of this book. In general, I have been less concerned with chronological rigidities than with a recreation of the man as I knew him—his work, his views of family and friends, his sensitivity as a person and artist, his beliefs, and his ideas.

If I seem to quote him with so much assurance, it is because I went home after seeing him and tried to jot down what he had said as nearly as I could remember it. In his case, I wanted to keep a record. Since Ernest's use of the spoken language was extremely uninhibited, I have tried to adhere to the obligations of a trusted friend in presenting his conversations. He loved to talk and talked at length about the things he believed in. Also he had a way of drawing out your opinions that made you feel as if you had really said something.

Ernest Hemingway was a man who lived many of the great abstractions he dramatized in fiction—love, truth, honor, loyalty, courage, humility, and pride. In

8

celebrating the Religion of Man, he formulated as rigid a set of rules for living and attaining manhood as can be found in any religion.

This little book, therefore, is an attempt to reduce the Hemingway legend to fact, insofar as my knowledge and understanding of the man permit; yet as discriminating as I have been, I think the legend, unfortunately as legends always do, will beat the truth in the end.

W. S.

Acknowledgments

For permission to quote from Ernest Hemingway's *A Moveable Feast*, I make grateful acknowledgment to Charles Scribner's Sons. I am also indebted to the following persons: Malcolm Cowley, Valerie Danby-Smith, Marlene Dietrich, Leicester Hemingway, Wallace Meyer, Eric Moorn, Robert W. Stallman, John Steinbeck, and Denis Zaphiro. Certainly I must place on the record that my greatest debt goes to Mary Hemingway for her understanding and generosity.

My Friend

ERNEST HEMINGWAY

I.

In late June of that year Mary Hemingway sent an unexpected message, "Papa is steadily improving . . . .Best regards." Exactly thirteen days later when my family and I walked into our home upon returning from a weekend trip, the telephone was ringing.

July 2, 1961, was a calm and beautiful Sunday in Virginia. How typical, I thought, for the telephone to be the herald of routine. Indeed, the pressures of work had made necessary a few days away from interruptions. Now after a very brief rest I expected the vicissitudes associated with home and work. But I was not prepared for this telephone call.

"Bill, have you heard the news?" exclaimed my nephew's voice at the other end. "Has your radio been on, or television?"

Informing him that we had been away and purposely out of touch with radio and other news media, I was benumbed by his next words.

"Ernest Hemingway shot himself early this morning!" Before I could reply, his voice quavered uncertainly,

15

"They don't know whether it was an accident or not." An avid sportsman himself, this young man had been a Hemingway fan since his late teens.

"Was the shot fatal?" I demanded sharply.

"I'm not sure but I think so." And with brief amenities he terminated our conversation.

Remembering the numerous close passes with death that Ernest had experienced over the years and especially recalling the front-page obituaries following his airplane crashes in Uganda near Murchison Falls in January 1954; I tried to make myself believe this was another episode from which his seemingly charmed life would again emerge, somewhat battered, perhaps, but intact.

Such, however, was not to be the case. Within the hour, special news broadcasts repeated the sad account of this unusual man's death. At first I was still dumbfounded, not really comprehending the finality voiced by the newcasters. The impact of what they reported did not hit me deeply at that moment. It took a while for that to happen.

Like Huck Finn, Ernest has been there before, I attempted to convince myself. There must be misinformation on the part of the networks. He'll pop up unexpectedly as he did in Africa. But this was a case of intuition trying to overrule reason.

Nevertheless, when I first accepted the fact that Ernest Hemingway was dead, my immediate thoughts went back to the note Mary had written us on their Christmas card mailed from Rochester, Minnesota, and dated December 19, 1960, saying they were at Mayo Clinic under another name and strictly a secret, so that Ernest might get a thorough examination and keep his bloood pressure down. She then went on to say that, so far, the examinations had optimistic results and they hoped to

16

return home early in the new year.

A month later I received what turned out to be Ernest's last letter to me. It gave the impression of his being in good spirits and having the blood pressure under control. Implying that he felt much improved, Ernest indicated his intention of leaving St. Mary's Hospital shortly and returning to Ketchum, Idaho, where he was most anxious to be. Although he was apparently a very sick man at that time, he made a gesture typical of his thoughtfulness and generosity—that of proffering a friendly gift. He would try to fly us a brace of fat mallard drakes in dry ice if the shooting season were not over.

As the news bulletins repeated themselves that peaceful Sunday evening in July, the one thing that haunted my consciousness was the recollection of the utter unselfishness of the man Hemingway and of his habitual concern for others. The impact of his unique individualism was such that it did not really occur to me then—and this must have been the initial reaction of all his friends—that the world had lost a writer of first magnitude, perhaps the most articulate practitioner of fiction of our century. To those who knew him well, Ernest was first and foremost a staunch and loyal friend.

For me, at least, the following week was a period of bewilderment. Frankly, since reading my first story of his in the late 1920's when I was a boy, it had never occurred to me that there might be a world in which Hemingway did not actually live. During the early stages of my awakening to this fact, however, the unreality of a world without Ernest Hemingway, that solid and indestructible rock, was almost uncanny. Perceptive individuals everywhere must have sensed that this planet would never be quite the same again. With his passing, as with the assassination of President John F. Kennedy two years later, the world lost something of its youth, its faith, and its vitality.

With the passage of time, memories continued to flood in of Ernest and our friendship. One memory led to another until my own life was recharged with the wisdom and devotion of this rare individual. These recollections were in direct contradiction to much of the drivel and sensationalism that littered newspapers and magazines, and was soon to appear between hard as well as soft covers. It was not long then until I knew someday I would have to write about my friend Ernest Hemingway.

II.

The last time I saw Ernest was in October 1957. In mid-September he and Mary had come to New York where he attended the championship prize fight in which Sugar Ray Robinson was defending his title against Carmen Basilio, and where he also took in part of the World's Series. At that time, considerable space in the press had been devoted to his health and to the strict diet his physicians had prescribed. Ernest told me later that he had just been given a thorough going over by his doctors, including his friend, the ship's doctor on the *Ile de France.*

On October 3, Ernest telephoned me from his New York hotel, saying they would be leaving for Miami two days later and invited me to join them in Washington. Knowing his aversion to using the telephone, I was particularly pleased that he took time when he was pressed by business, obligations to other friends, and a generally tight schedule.

I met Ernest and Mary at Union Station, Washington, D. C., on the afternoon of Saturday, October 5. They

19

had a Pullman on the deluxe Seaboard Silver Star. Ernest bounced down the Pullman steps like a schoolboy, then walked on the balls of his feet to the platform, all the while keeping an intense smile. As usual he was electrodynamic but in complete control. The thought occurred to me, as it had before, here's a man who has stayed young because he always has somewhere to go. He symbolizes enjoyment of life and infects others with his own sense of well-being.

Ernest appeared to be in the peak of health and was in excellent spirits. His marvelous coloration contrasted happily with his neatly-trimmed white beard and almost-white head of thick hair. Wearing a well-fitting, double-breasted, dark suit with white shirt and plain necktie which matched his suit, Ernest looked imposing because of his heavy shoulders, deep chest, and his long, solid arms. His weight was down to almost two hundred pounds, he was to inform me later in the trip, confessing, "While I was off alcohol, I lost twenty-five pounds."

On the station platform outside their Pullman, Ernest and Mary chatted with a couple of friends who had come to see them en route. Mary had spent the night in Washington.

"Bill Seward is my loyal friend who never lets me down," Ernest said to them. With his hand on my shoulder, he added with a chuckle, "Whenever everybody else says Dr. Hemingstein is on the skids, Bill Seward sticks by me." As a youngster, by the way, Ernest had written features for his high school paper in the manner of Ring Lardner under the name of Hemingstein. He always seemed to get a big kick out of applying this designation jokingly to himself in conversation with friends during later years.

Inside the Hemingway New York-Miami Pullman,
October 1957. (Photos by Denis Zaphiro)

Joseph Papp, Producer of "New York Shakespeare Festival."
(1965-1966, 1967) (Photos by Friedman-Abeles)

There was some talk of art and baseball. Then someone brought up the subject of the first Russian sputnik, which had gone into orbit the day before.

Playfully, Ernest mimicked the talk he had overheard in New York the previous night:

" 'Let's make peace now! Let's make peace!' People are saying." Almost immediately his mood became serious.

Departure time had arrived. After an exchange of good-bye's, Ernest, Mary, and I boarded the Hemingway Pullman. Inside I was introduced to Denis Zaphiro, a young Englishman who was a game-warden in Kenya and a guest of the Hemingways, who were giving him his first sight of the East Coast of the United States. Shortly, Zaphiro retired to his private room and Ernest suggested we have a drink. Remembering what some of the New York columnists had recently printed about his being strictly on non-alcoholic drinks by doctors' orders, I must have appeared momentarily puzzled, because Mary exclaimed, "For writers we drink very little, you know."

Ernest opened one of the several large leather bags sitting in their drawing room. It was filled with new magazines and a large assortment of whisky bottles. Mary indicated she preferred a martini, Ernest as usual selected Scotch, and I took bourbon. As was his practice with friends, Ernest offered a genial toast and we drank to each other and to Mary.

Then, looking at his wrist watch and remembering a World's Series game was in progress, he turned on his transistor radio. The announcer's voice came clear and strong. For some time Ernest indulged in one of the most subtly authoritative discourses I had ever heard on the intricacies of professional baseball; yet spoken in a fashion that suggested no superior knowledge—a characteristic, incidentally, he normally displayed in the company of those he liked. During the next short period, I am sure I learned as much about the idiosyncrasies of individual players on both teams as I could have by studying carefully an encyclopedia of baseball or a who's who in sports.

Frequently his attention was drawn away from baseball to things suggested by places outside. Military installations particularly aroused his enthusiasm and I well remember the perceptive comments and questions he posed when the train passed the marine base at Quantico. This veteran of five wars began talking of what he called "the science of war" and of specific wars of one kind or another. A pronouncement of Ernest's made years earlier flashed across my memory with lightning speed:

"An aggressive war is the great crime against everything good in the world," he had written. "A defensive war, which must necessarily turn to aggressive at the earliest moment, is the great counter-crime. But never think that war, no matter how necessary, nor how justified is not a crime."

It was not long before the battlefields outside Fredericksburg came into sight. Observing the dense forests, thick undergrowth, and irregular elevation, Ernest made a number of cogent remarks relating to terrain and its effects upon battle strategy; also spontaneous observations about the impact wooded areas, bodies of water, and geographical phenomena in general can have upon weather. This was all particularized information you might have expected from a professional meteorological specialist.

We pointed our remarks more specifically to aspects of the Fredericksburg Campaign itself. As I found to be true with so many subjects, Ernest's detailed knowledge

22

of that remote slaughter was amazing. Then, in the midst of our discussion of the battle, neither of us was certain about a picayunish point that came up. Ernest leaned close to my ear and almost whispered, wryly, "We know the law but not the canon."

Later when we were eating in the dining car, Mary turned to Ernest and asked, "Papa, did you go to the bank yesterday?"

He nodded.

"Did they try to sell you anything?" she continued.

"Yes," Ernest added, "they always try to sell you something. Anything they try to sell you is something they want to get rid of."

Years later after his death, I read a published account of his investment portfolio. Unlike the public image of a man who led the life of great risks he wrote about, Ernest did not attempt the dramatic as an investor. According to reports, based on an accounting filed in 1964 with the New York State Tax Commission, Ernest left stocks and bonds with major holdings of sizeable shares in Eastman Kodak, General Motors, Bethlehem Steel, and American Telephone and Telegraph. His choice of comparatively conservative stocks may appear out of character but they made good sense for a writer, even with his predictable royalties. Thinking back, I recalled what he had said to Mary on the train that day about bankers and brokers.

Back in their drawing room, Mary attempted to take a nap, informing us that she was exhausted from late hours the preceding night. All the while except for eating, Ernest and I had been sipping our drinks rather steadily—if slowly—and by now concentrated our talk upon literature and his own writing, a subject Ernest seldom indulged in voluntarily.

23

"Bill, you are my shortstop whom I admire," he said, looking straight at me with his interested eyes. "Anyone can play second or third base, but a good shortstop is hard to come by."

Enunciating slowly and with great seriousness, he continued the baseball imagery, which was always a favorite metaphorical habit with him.

"You don't see me as a literary man now. As you know, when I'm on vacation like this, I stay completely away from writing. But when I'm writing, I do nothing else. I'm like a pitcher—am in there to win and work at it every minute of the way."

After a brief pause he added, "I always work on a story right up until it is published."

The next moment Ernest said with circumspection, "Not long ago I filled out a questionnaire which will appear in the next issue of *The Paris Review*. They will probably misquote me, as they usually do."

Several months later he sent me a copy of that number of *The Paris Review* from San Francisco de Paula, Cuba. Typically, he had thought to inscribe it warmly.

After I had quizzed him about his writing habits and clarified several points of literary theory, Ernest said with professional pride, *"The Atlantic Monthly* people have asked me for two stories to use in their one hundredth anniversary issue."

With deliberation he continued slowly, *"The Atlantic,* you know, published my first story in this country."

I gestured my knowledge of this fact.

"The stories I have sent them represent the two extremes in my writing," he added enthusiastically. "The first is tough as a story can be. Many readers won't like it. Remember the old story, 'The Light of the World'?

"It's rough like that, a good story for those who like whores," adding in almost a whisper, "Mary understands what I mean. The other story is the exact opposite—as delicate as they come."

After I had expressed interest in the forthcoming *Atlantic* pieces, Ernest continued, "I think my next book will be a book of stories. Have almost enough now. Am working on a book about Africa but have to go back there to make sure of a few details." The latter remark, of course, reflected his usual scrupulosity as an artist.

In this context he mentioned, without elaboration, his recent intense work on what he called "my Paris sketches," a volume that turned out to be the posthumously-published *A Moveable Feast.*

Almost in the same breath Ernest brought up the subject of a neo-gothic novel of mine, *Skirts of the Dead Night,* which had come out several years earlier. Soon after its publication Ernest had written me in haste that he thought it "excellent" and added, "I'll write you about your book which I liked greatly." As a matter of fact, while the story had been in the process of composition, he had indicated his willingness to read it in manuscript or in proof or between stiff covers, saying I could count on him to do whatever I wanted him to.

Not wishing to capitalize upon a friendship, I never followed up his offer, though I did send him a copy of the novel after it was published. And so, on an October day a few years later, Ernest said to me, "Your novel was good. I enjoyed it. I didn't write you in detail about it because I am not a critic." In tone and in context, his remark seemed more genuinely complimentary than even the most favorable printed reviews this novel had received.

A few minutes later Ernest said in amused undertones

25

that a well-known fountain pen company had recently sent him one of their pens and offered him $10,000 just to use his picture in an advertisement—no written statement, no endorsement, only his picture.

"I couldn't get the damned pen to write and so didn't answer their letter."

Pausing momentarily, he added with boyish glee, "Several months later I saw Carl Sandburg's picture in one of their ads. Sandburg must have got his pen to write."

Denis Zaphiro came in. After I expressed a few pleasantries in deference to the British, he seemed flattered and then talked a bit about his duties as game-warden. In a little while he took pictures of Ernest, Mary, and me. The mention of pictures brought on a detectable tense reflex in Ernest. It was easy to sense the apparent physical and psychological pain this man experienced in front of a camera, even with friends. He was to tell me later on, as no doubt he also confided to others, that to him the click of a camera was like the rattle of a snake.

His life-long hatred of any kind of personal publicity, whether the printed word or photography, may not be too widely recognized. Yet any newspaper man who knew Ernest must be quite aware of this fact. He would neither willingly pose nor talk about his books or himself for them. But it was different when it came to those he trusted. With them he was a fine companion—thoughtful, generous, and considerate. As Denis Zaphiro was to say, "Papa posed with you as a friend but he would have refused to have his picture taken if you had been a newspaper man."

"Luck" was always a favorite word of Ernest's as it was, incidentally, of Mark Twain's. The word appears frequently in the published works of both men. But Ernest used it not infrequently in conversation and, interestingly, often knocked on wood for emphasis. Even concerning truly great writing, he had long ago penned the observation that *it* might be achieved if an author works hard enough and "has luck."

As the porter was leaving after having brought more ice for our drinks, Ernest insisted with feeling that he wanted to see him for sure before we debarked. Perhaps noting my puzzled expression, Ernest said something that I have never forgotten: "If you want people to be polite to you, you have to be twice as polite to them."

With the porter gone, we started another drink, our conversation drifting to the subject of racial integration (a somewhat delicate topic in the South at that time). I told him a few of the things being done in the Commonwealth of Virginia and mentioned also some of the things I felt were not being done properly. As he was prone to do, Ernest particularized the dialogue by referring to several longtime friends who were Negro musicians.

"All of them are dead except one," he said, commenting briefly upon his last meeting with the latter.

"So you see, Bill, I've had integration all along." Then he immediately changed the subject.

Before we parted, Ernest insisted that I let him do some favor for me. "Do you have any books you want me to inscribe? Is there anything you'd like me to do for you?"

I reminded him that he had sent me inscribed copies of several of his novels and, therefore, I certainly did not wish to appear selfish and impose upon his good nature.

"But," I added, "my two daughters would love to have your autograph."

27

Smiling, he took a piece of paper from one of his pockets and wrote a warm inscription to each of these girls: "To Jenny—With all good wishes always—Hope we will have the good luck to meet you soon," for the older; and "To Leigh—from her friend," for the younger; both signed "Ernest Hemingway."

Much later, as we left the train, Ernest introduced me to the conductor, saying with almost innocent enthusiasm and with an appreciative twinkle, "Mr. Seward teaches my books in his classes at William and Mary College."* Ernest could not have seemed prouder had he been a novice and I the first person to take note of his work.

As we parted, Ernest gave me a bear-hug and an emphatic invitation to my family and myself to visit them soon at Finca Vigia. On the Norfolk-bound plane it occurred to me again, as it had a number of times since I first came to know Ernest, that he was the only great man I ever met who was not a disappointment in the flesh. On the contrary, Ernest always seemed larger than life: invincible as a man, a giant in both his personal letters and published works.

*The College of William and Mary in Norfolk became Old Dominion College in 1962, and Old Dominion University in 1969.

III.

Hemingway's friendship with the famous among professional military men, movie stars, columnists, maharajahs, athletes, toreros, restaurateurs, and others has been publicized for years. Hating publicity intensely, Ernest over a long period of time refused to give out any information about his personal life and friendships. Lacking what they considered adequate data, many newsmen made up episodes, adventures, people, places, and relationships. Mistaken for fact, countless of these rumors contributed to the Hemingway legend and already they have become part of literary history. But contrary to this public image, Ernest always liked little people as much as he did big people.

Looking back, I find it somewhat hard to realize that my initial contact with Ernest came about as a result of my growing professional interest in his works as they related to contemporary American literature in general. As a young college teacher of twentieth-century fiction I had written him of my respect and enthusiasm for his prose. His reply, dated March 10, 1940, came from Hotel

Ambos Mundos in Havana. With generous but unsentimental expression of appreciation, Ernest concluded this first communication with the same thought which characterized his last direct word to me from his sick bed in Rochester, Minnesota: a voluntary offer of a gift. Having stated some specific facts about the progress of a novel he was then working on, he added that when it came out, he would like to send me an inscribed copy. And he did. The book, of course, was *For Whom the Bell Tolls,* published in October of that year. He had asserted in the letter that if he had luck, it would be much the best novel he had written. As far as I know, Ernest always considered this to be his finest single book.

During the ensuing months the war in Europe became steadily more virulent. Ernest and his new wife, Martha Gellhorn, a correspondent for *Collier's,* were observing first-hand the Sino-Japanese War. Soon there was to be Pearl Harbor. Thus, with the complication of events around the world and Ernest's own propensity for travel and involvement, I heard almost nothing from him directly for almost three years. Then came rather sporadic communications through the mid-1940's.

Having known a number of poets and writers of fiction since my early undergraduate days and accepting the general opinion that artists are not particularly noted for making friends, I had little reason in those days to expect anything from the famous author of *A Farewell to Arms* but a professional exchange of ideas and impressions. How little I then knew about the man Hemingway! Nevertheless, our early letters possessed a special rapport that was to develop after a few years to the point that I, like his other friends, became one of those who considered him their own private property.

30

Even Marlene Dietrich, who called Ernest "the most fascinating man I know," regarded him as her "personal Rock of Gibraltar." What I did not know in those early days was Ernest's unique capacity for making and retaining friends.

As our association grew, the ambience which was his special trademark became more and more evident. Always the man of action (and the writer who composed the gospel of action), Ernest had been accident-prone from childhood. It did not take too long, however, to discover in this adventurer-hunter-fisherman an individual who was generous and tolerant in his estimates of others. I learned that he respected most of all loyalty, kindness, integrity, and courage; he hated treachery, self-seeking, and fakery.

During the last year or two of the war, a letter of mine was now and then delayed in the mails. He would later say playfully of such a document that he did not know what could have held it up so long unless it was that the censor did not agree with my opinion of his published works.

In those months we shared opinions of books and writing, as well as of authors. He seemed pleased with this exchange, confessing there was little talk of books where he was. He had been rereading *War and Peace* in the then new Aylmar Maude translation, which he respected a great deal. Indeed, Ernest's high regard for the towering nineteenth-century Russian writers of fiction is well known. When I informed him that I was using *Crime and Punishment* in one of my college courses, he seemed quite pleased. Then complimenting *The Brothers* and *The Idiot,* he alluded to *The Gambler,* saying he always thought it was a "wonderful story too."

Of the novels by young Americans at war, *Tucker's*

31

People appeared to capture his enthusiasm and prompted his conclusion that Ira Wolfert should be capable of producing a marvelous novel after the war. Ernest also told me in the summer of 1943, that he had not written anything since the Introduction to *Men at War,* which he had finished a year earlier, but that he had learned enough at what he had been doing to make a good book.

A bit earlier I had called Ernest's attention to a volume of criticism by Joseph Warren Beach, *American Fiction, 1920-1940,* that contained what I considered an excellent commentary on his major works. Not having seen the book, Ernest appeared definitely interested and asked if I would let him see my copy. Later, he confided that he thought Beach's book was extremely favorable to him but seemed spotty in its criticism of other writers who could have been treated more justly. Then he added that criticism always puzzled him but he liked to read it in case it had something he should know.

By 1943, incidentally, Ernest began to type letters, spacing three or four times between words   so   that it   looked   like   this   when   written   down. This was a longtime habit of his when writing books and letters that "counted." As is fairly well known, Ernest did   this   to   slow   himself   down   and   emphasize   the importance of each word. In like manner, he spoke slowly and deliberately whenever he engaged in serious conversation, as if measuring the impact of every word.

During World War II Ernest had stayed at sea on the *Pilar* for close to two years expecting to fight every day, then had flown combat missions in Europe, and finally had spent one hundred five days in a very dangerous undertaking during the liberation of France. Of course, as always, some people accused him of publicity seeking. I well remember his somewhat bewildered observation

32

years later to the effect that, in his opinion, only "a limited amount of people" would have done these things for publicity. Even Evelyn Waugh, who certainly should have been better informed, announced that Ernest was bitter because he had been unable to take an official part in the war and had to serve as a correspondent.

IV.

A gaudy, uneven, and gossipy book of memoirs of American expatriates in Paris was published in 1947. Entitled *Paris Was Our Mistress,* the book was written by Samuel Putnam, a fairly well-known critic and editor who claimed to be an observer of the American colony there during the 1920's and 1930's. His account contained extended portraits and impressions of Ernest Hemingway, Gertrude Stein, and Ezra Pound. Responding to something I had written about it, Ernest found the book a strange mixture of good intention, inaccurate journalism, and personal alibis for some pretty strange things this man had done in his time. He mentioned the repeated attacks Putnam had made in the Communist press on *For Whom the Bell Tolls* but confessed that the reader gets no idea of this in Putnam's book, adding in a low key that Putnam was a very slippery character who, in Paris, had a fine subject to write on.

As events developed, the spring and summer of 1947, were rugged months for the Hemingways. In mid-April,

Ernest's middle boy, Patrick, had a severe (and unattended) concussion in an automobile accident in Key West. The boy was not put to bed but played six sets of tennis with his younger brother, Gregory, instead and kept up his exercise without taking any rest until he was in bad condition when he got back to Finca Vigía. Patrick was critically ill for five months, during which period Ernest spent full time looking after him.

Meanwhile, Mary had to go to Chicago where her father underwent surgery. Shortly after returning to Cuba, she developed severe flu with complications resulting in a fever close to 104 for two weeks in spite of treatment with the various sulphas and finally was put on penicillin.

Afterwards the doctors found Ernest had high blood pressure and corresponding overweight. After months of working diligently at getting his weight down and the pressure with it, he managed to bring the weight just below two hundred ten pounds and the blood pressure down in proportion.

When Patrick had turned up in such bad shape, Ernest was 130,000 words into a novel, rewriting and cutting on the first section, and almost ready to get into the new part again. But the illnesses of his wife and son threw him several months behind with the novel. The fact is, much of his writing career suffered interruptions resulting from wars, wounds, accidents to himself or members of his family as well as from self-imposed excursions. Ernest had expressed something of this for publication in the third person in 1936: "Since he was a young boy he has cared greatly for fishing and shooting. If he had not spent so much time at them, at ski-ing, at the bull ring, and in a boat, he might have written much more."

35

In August, 1948, Ernest wrote again about the book in progress, saying he thought it would be good, "But every time it is harder to beat the last one when you write each time to the complete fulfilling of how well you can write." He seemed to attribute his increased difficulty to the fact that he was trying to beat what he had written instead of to equal or repeat his own former writing. In this general context Ernest ventured his opinion that pace is almost as important as good taste in a writer. Nobody can last in life but, according to him, writers do not last at all if they have no sense of pace.

Referring to his own writing, he stated matter-of-factly that people were getting to see it was good although lots of commentators tried to prove the opposite, and had for many years. Sometimes he reread his own stories to cheer himself up, confessing that at such times he wondered "how the hell any son of a bitch could write that well." Typically, he added, "That isn't conceit. It is knowing my trade."

At intervals during the coming years, Ernest expressed his gratitude to me for having detected the strengths in his fiction. He seemed particularly pleased that I continued to write him—such letters, he said, made him happy when he needed to be made so. In fact in 1948, he wrote of the letters, "They always come to me with the fine clean feeling of loyalty; the feeling you get with good grain you pick a handful up from the bin and sift through your hand."

About that time he suggested that his former wife had fallen into the trap of ambition, noting that she probably had had it all along. He seemed to feel that being so popular at war had been too much for her judgment. Alluding to some of her then recent pieces, Ernest intimated that she was perfectly capable of

36

writing a good book. This is the only direct reference that Ernest ever made to me concerning Martha Gellhorn after their divorce. She, of course, was to marry T. S. Matthews (later divorced), settle in London, and continue her career as journalist and writer of fiction.

Ernest, himself, indulged in journalism now and then during the decade, producing among other articles a particularly fine one in *Holiday* just before 1950. He always made a real distinction between journalism and serious fiction, stating at one point, "All journalism is movable [*sic*] feast."

For almost ten years we had exchanged ideas and opinions about the great French technicians in fiction and the important nineteenth-century Russian novelists, some of whom I had assigned to students in my college courses in literature—notably Flaubert, Dostoyevsky, and Tolstoy. In the late 1940's when I informed Ernest that I used *A Farewell to Arms* as required reading, he seemed delighted. The student edition contained a rather detailed introduction by Robert Penn Warren. Commenting upon Warren's introduction, Ernest indicated that he considered it a good one as far as introductions go. Having used one or more of his books in my advanced courses in twentieth-century fiction over the years, I introduced a Senior Seminar in Ernest Hemingway for English majors after his death. When I wrote Mary about this seminar in 1962, and of how enthusiastically the students responded after studying Ernest's works, she appeared grateful and pleased, replying it seemed incredible to her that she couldn't "turn to Papa and say, 'Did you see what Bill Seward says about his senior course on You?' "

Apropos of using novels in college courses, I recall John Steinbeck's contrasted view regarding the teaching

37

of his books, for he said to me once, "Please don't make your students read my work. This could give them a hatred they would never outgrow. If you want them to read my work—forbid it. Then they will not only read it but will have a fine sense of sin too and some triumph over authority."

By mid-summer 1949, Ernest was hard at work again on the novel, or as he put it working "at full manifold pressure" which tired him to the point that he had "nothing left." In August he recited his weekly yield, which had decreased slightly during the later weeks, but which averaged out quite well for him. Ernest's own terse comment perhaps best reveals how he evaluated his own writing output then: "The law of diminishing returns but returns still good." Coincidentally, I was well into the final draft of my own novel, which Ernest had insisted would be "a very great pleasure" for him to read.

A well-known critic had an uninformed piece in *The New York Times* about Ernest, published a few months earlier. Referring to his printed reply to such a comic performance, Ernest admitted to me that he ran over the critic with a bulldozer and the reviewer thought it was "elusive." Also the novelist was a bit irked by a reference to his "extravagant" life. After enumerating the many times he had been wounded, the number of men he had killed in combat, the five wars he had served in, and a few other dangerous actions he had participated in, Ernest declared ironically that these might make a man a little bit "extravagant."

V.

The Hemingway legend tends to obscure the fact of Ernest's susceptibility to illnesses, accidents, and infections over the years. By his own admission he had been running into hard luck in the very late 1940's and into 1950. 1949 and 1950 were particularly bad years with regard to sickness and accidents. He was near death in Padova of combined erysipelas, streptococcus, and strepholococcus with anthrax from the hair of gun wadding. But by June 1950, Ernest had pretty well recovered. There was a school of thought at the time that he had cancer of the throat and skin. Fortunately, it turned out there was nothing malignant, though for some time he had had a bothersome, benign skin nonsense which permitted him to shave only every few months and had caused him much anxiety. This chronic skin ailment is the chief explanation for the full beard he maintained during the last years of his life.

On July the first, however, he slipped coming over the rail on the flying bridge of *Pilar* in a very heavy sea just as the mate swung the boat to enter a channel. Hanging

39

onto the rail with one hand and suddenly striking the top of his head against the clamps which hold the huge Marlin gaffs, Ernest suffered a cut into the skull and a severed artery, resulting in a concussion. As was not usual with him, several hours elapsed before the cut was sewed up. On top of this, while chasing some cattle thieves who had broken into his property at San Francisco de Paula the following night, he slipped, and trying to protect his head, injured his bad leg and what he regarded as his good one. The doctors treated his right ankle and leg with massage but X-rays revealed seven pieces of shell fragment in the right calf. The fall had apparently torn them loose in such a way that one was resting on a vein and another touching a nerve. Also there were eleven fragments of metal and one bullet in the left calf.

All of this, as Ernest was to say, "played hell" with his writing and his correspondence. I mention these details because they illustrate the adverse writing conditions that plagued him off and on for years, and they served as a real test for his forbearance, especially regarding personal publicity. As he was to write me later, he did not want to tell anyone about the accidents because many critics and observers would have thought it was a "publicity thing."

Since it was about the time that *Across the River and into the Trees* came out, the author was pretty fed up with some of the silly stuff which was already being printed about him and the book. I can imagine his real annoyance had the press learned of those accidents and tried to make something of them. Luckily, the news media knew nothing of his illnesses and, as a result, they were unable to invent anything this time.

I did get the impression he was put out with some of his

hostile critics when they became extremely vocal in their accusations that he was prostituting himself to *Cosmopolitan,* which as the record shows, had already published "The Short Happy Life of Francis Macomber," "Under the Ridge," "One Trip Across," as well as two or three other fine stories. Like a youngster who had outwitted his adversary, Ernest appeared amused, and even pleased, that "some son of a bitch" who hated him and did not understand his works had paid money to buy a stamp in order to call him a prostitute.

"Have been a lot of things," he mused, "but never that."

On the other hand, he was keenly appreciative of "fighting guys" who wrote to tell him what the book meant to them. He was especially moved, I think, by the remark of a British Lieutenant General whom he had known in Italy when they were very young men. Concerning the military aspects of the novel, his friend wrote, "Hem, how do you know things that only I know? When did you learn about sorrow and why did you never tell me?" Then a Venetian novelist, who was not given to making compliments, said of *Across the River,* "Nobody ever wrote about Venice before and now nobody will ever be able to write about it again." After that I do not think Ernest paid much serious attention to the seeming critical collusion against the book.

About the same time, I had complained to him of one particular unjust review of my own novel and his reply, it always seemed to me, reflected his mature judgment regarding criticism, "We all get bad reviews and you have to take them just as a fighter has to take a punch." In the same letter he admitted he used to get angry when reviews were stupid, untrue, or envious. Then looking back over the years, I became acutely aware that Ernest

41

had received more than his share of backhanded and prejudicial reviews written out of envy. There is, after all, one undeniable fact of human nature: excellence inspires envy.

Knowing I was committed to review *Across the River* professionally, Ernest told me some time before its publication that he thought I would like the book.

"But," he added, "knock the bejeesus out of it if you don't. You can damn it to hell and still be my good friend."

This is a fairly typical illustration of the attitude Ernest took toward reviewers when he thought they were sincere and honest in their judgments. Unlike a number of critics who attacked *Across the River* when it came out (many have since had second thoughts and have reevaluated it in a calmer frame of mind), I found the story a tremendous emotional experience and much of the author's writing as good as ever, an opinion I have had no reason to change.

Upon publication of *Across the River* I wrote, in part:

> The novel is one of mood, impeccably projected. A tender and moving love story, it is at the same time a powerful indictment of the shamefulness of war. Some readers will not like what Hemingway has to say about the allied general officers in the recent war, nor will they, in all probability, agree with him concerning what makes a good soldier good. Hemingway has always been uncompromising in exploring the truth as he sees it, and this novel, as well as his other books, is a strong and perhaps unpalatable dose for timid readers suffering from mental inertia.
>
> Superficially, the novel is deceptively simple in structure. The technique which Hemingway employs, however, is extremely difficult and it imposes technical problems that only the most skillful writer

could manage. Chief among these problems is the handling of time, at best always one of the most difficult elements in the successful writing of prose fiction. In *Across the River and into the Trees* time is even more compressed than it is in Joyce's *Ulysses.* The story is centered upon a microcosm of action, the author making marvelous use of the stream-of-consciousness device and the method of memory recall.

It is greatly to Hemingway's credit that he is able to recreate the horror and shame of war by means of retrospection. The fighting is over; the reader hears only its echoes (almost unbearable echoes.) And it can safely be said that none of the young novelists emerging from World War II has written as truthfully or as powerfully of war as Hemingway has in this new novel. Too many of the G. I.'s who have written of the last war have been interested primarily in the injustices done to themselves. Hemingway is an artist writing about the unhappy science of war.

Since I was aware that Ernest never subscribed to a clipping agency, I sent him a copy of my published review. He immediately expressed his deep appreciation, coincidentally alluding to reviewers who had attacked the book, saying, in effect, the hell with it. "If they don't understand this book that's their hard luck. You've understood it and some one else will." He also intimated that most of the reviews he had seen were silly but that his writer-friend from Venice commented that my piece was "the only intelligent criticism he read."

But most of all, he seemed happy that I liked the book. Here again is a side of the man the public knew little of. The fact that I had enjoyed the story meant more to him than a printed review which was mainly favorable. Ernest perhaps best summed up his feeling in a longhand postscript: "Thank you very much again for liking the book. I like it too!" Personally, I have always felt that *Across the River* (dedicated to Mary) had a very special and personal significance for him.

As I recall, the final reference Ernest made about *Across the River* was in connection with the highly perceptive full-page review in *The London Times Literary Supplement.* He even took the trouble to get a copy from London and sent it to me.

I am confident he felt rather nonplussed over the general critical reception of the book but pleased with the sales even though the novel was not submitted to any book club. It is understandable that Ernest thought a man who had written as well as he could for thirty years, who had always fought for his country and what he believed in, and who had been wounded many times in the process, would have been highly respected in any other country. In truth, he was to explain his reaction to critics of *Across the River* by saying he did not feel egotistical, only amazed.

"The first experience I had with those people," he told me, speaking of critics, "was a man named Ernest Walsh who wanted to publish *The Sun Also Rises* in a magazine called *This Quarter.* He had read it in manuscript and wrote me how much he liked it, etc. I explained that I had a publication date and so couldn't serialize when his magazine was coming out irregularly."

According to Ernest, when *The Sun Also Rises* came out, Walsh reviewed it as "The Cheapest Book I Ever Read."

Thus at mid-century the novelist's last words on "those people" were, "Well, the hell with them. Don't let them ever get you down and I will not either."

VI.

The year 1951 was all work for Ernest. Instead of whining over the critical massacre of *Across the River*, he kept hard at work on *The Old Man and the Sea*. As far as I am aware, the only reference to book reviewing then was it seemed pretty bad to him, asserting that he did not think his view was completely conditioned by what most of the reviewers had said about *Across the River*. Maybe it was, but he thought there was more to it than that. For any reasonable person, it would have been hard to take issue with his expression of discouragement over the general state of book reviewing.

Frankly, the image which the press continued to perpetuate tended to obscure the fact that Hemingway was first and foremost a literary man—a writer and reader. Literature was never far from his mind, a truth that must have prompted Gertrude Stein's reference of long ago that he was "a man of museums."

All through the year Ernest was writing at what he thought to be his best and he confided that he was also having great luck with his work. His health remained good except for an attack of flu in February, a persistent skin infection, and a couple of broken ribs in the fall. By the end of the year his blood pressure was down to 136/68, which was almost half what it had been a few years earlier and which, for him, was supposed to have been very good.

With respect to his writing, reports from Finca Vigia had continued on a happy note to the year's end. Ernest had written the third and fourth books of a novel, having already rewritten and cut the second book. With only a little checking over, the last two could have gone to the printers at that time. 1951 ended with the book standing at 183,251 words, although he felt the need of a vacation so that he could come back to it and see it fresh, filling in where it needed any of that and cutting anything that could come out. That is, Ernest was still doing the usual job he always had done on such parts. Much later, he is reputed to have said that *The Old Man and the Sea* was a coda: "an epilogue to a long book. Like a dog's tail. Then I threw away the dog and used the tail."

This sort of reading over and meticulous revision was always part of the Hemingway stock-in-trade. I remember his comment in the midst of the final proofing of *Across the River* that it almost literally killed him every time he read it, which was then over two hundred times, interjecting, "Well, as we say in Montana: 'you hired out to be tough, didn't you?' So I guess I can read it again."

About that time and while his writing was still going good, somebody sent Ernest a batch of books to autograph. It involved his paying a man to get the books through customs as well as having to pay several dollars' customs charges on his own works, which were to be

46

autographed as a favor. In addition, sending them back entailed tying up Ernest's chauffeur, who had to stand in line and get a permit at the ministry. Yet the real irony of such an importunate incident was that most of the books were first editions which Ernest, himself, did not even own.

Before becoming a part of the Writer's Conference at the University of Connecticut that summer, I had had a letter from its director, Robert W. Stallman, in April in which he went on to say: "I had written Ernest Hemingway to ask whether he might be in the States in December, on chance of his talking at M. L. A., for I've scheduled Contemporary Literature section to deal with Hemingway. And in a most interesting letter, full of personal material, he mentioned you, saying you know 'what I'm trying to do.' "

It was particularly heartening, I have to admit, to have Ernest's opinion of my judgment of his works confirmed second-hand by way of Connecticut. As things turned out, we had a good time of it at the conference with Stallmam, Malcolm Cowley, Oscar Williams, and Caroline Gordon (among others) hashing over contemporary American literature, the works of Hemingway in particular.

Since Ernest had been working "at full manifold pressure" throughout the year, there were months of silence in our correspondence—a situation that was perfectly natural on both our parts. As far as I was concerned, the intermission did not really matter, because I knew he was always there to hear from. In truth, I do not recall ever having asked him for advice *per se,* though his letters contained things that were useful for whatever problems I may have had. Thus he often helped without even knowing my problems at the

47

time. In this connection, one of his longtime famous friends commented that Ernest said remarkable things which seemed to adjust automatically to problems of all sizes.

Like a perceptive parent who senses the child's potential and nourishes the talent, Ernest helped and encouraged deserving young writers throughout his career. Specifically, this was the period when he established a prize in Poland, an award to be given the most promising young writer each year. He did the same thing in Italy, in each case using the local royalties from one or another of his books as the base money for the prizes, which continue to exist. This habit of his, I am confident, has never been generally known.

In 1953, Scribners brought out a volume called *The Hemingway Reader,* a representative selection of the author's works, edited by Charles Poore who also contributed excellent introductions to the stories. When his own editors first proposed it, Ernest suggested they get Joseph Warren Beach, Malcolm Cowley, Charles Poore, or me to do the introductions.

"There was no particular order in the suggestion," he was to write me later in a typical gesture of thoughtfulness. "They chose Charlie Poore. He has always known what I was trying to do and I think it was a good choice. But I thought you might be interested to know that you had been nominated. Probably, like Adlai Stevenson, you are very happy to know you didn't have to serve."

Within the year a strange book built up upon the premise that Hemingway was a victim of traumatic neurosis caused him to remark that he thought amateur psychoanalysts have as little right to ascribe neuroses to living people as amateur doctors have the right to publish

48

that a person has syphilis.

I had the impression Ernest thought the book rather ridiculous in its psychopathic arrogance, although he indicated that he would gladly try to learn anything its author had to teach him if the critic had ever fought, or if he could write, or if he could actually think clearly. But Ernest was convinced that the man could not even read a map or navigate. Ernest also observed there was quite convincing proof, between covers, that he could not write. On the face of things, he must have thought this critic would probably not have bled blood, but footnotes or phrases from his analyst, if shot.

Ernest's overall reaction to the book, which received some notoriety and to-be-expected acclaim from many academic critics, was that its author wrote somewhat like a jealous girl who loves you but, when she has a few drinks, tells you what a bastard you are, getting the accusations quite confused and, to make you angry, accusing you of all the things that are untrue. It might be mentioned, by the way, that the critic sent Ernest the book, presumably with a dedication. But Ernest had read the volume already and returned him his copy in its original wrapping.

The novelists's health had been basically good for nearly two years, his blood pressure still holding at approximately 130/64 without medication. That non-malignant skin ailment continued to be a nuisance. However, he no longer suffered the comparatively bad headaches that plagued him after World War II. As I recollect, the headaches had ceased around 1948. Anyhow, in 1953, Hemingway the writer felt he was way ahead on work but endeavored, as always, to pace himself.

It was harder to write all the time instead of easier, he

felt, but that was to be expected. At that period, according to his own diagnosis, he had to destroy the facility he had in order to achieve control.

VII.

The following was a memorable year for Ernest, its cumulative impact having been almost like a Georgia Sothern finale, though its effect, of course, was far from ecdysiastic. Following the two airplanes crashes in Africa in January, he read his own front-page obituaries in the world press. At the time he was so concerned for Mary that he did not tell anyone he was hurt. Yet it was discovered later that his injuries from the crashes were severe and had gone for a considerable time with little or no attention. The truth, I suspect, is that Ernest never fully recovered from the African crashes.

Not having heard from him since just before he and Mary left home for Africa and not knowing his whereabouts following the accidents, I attempted to contact him through Wallace Meyer, who was then his editor at Scribners. On March 1, 1954, Meyer advised me that Ernest was to sail from Mombasa on March 10, his destination being Venice.

It had been my hope to see him in New York upon his return, for in May he was due to receive the Award

51

of Merit given by the American Academy of Arts and Letters for distinguished fiction. The after effects of his accidents, however, imposed a longer period of recuperation than was expected and, after going to Madrid for the fiesta of San Isidro in May, Ernest and Mary sailed from Genoa early in June, proceeding directly to Cuba.

In one of his letters about Ernest, Wallace Meyer had said, "I recall especially your discerning review of *Across the River and into the Trees,* and I remember the satisfaction he found in your critical insight."

Ernest's failure to appear at the Academy's award presentation was not unusual. Some of us have always known that Ernest did not honor easily. He invariably welcomed action, often having gone out of his way to seek it. But for him, praise was a different matter entirely. A friend of his youth once said of Ernest, "After danger is over, he fades out of the picture."

Like all preeminent men, Ernest was aware of his own greatness. Personally, I am convinced he never felt any real need for public praise or awards. His satisfaction as a writer of fiction came from a knowledge that people read his stories, enjoyed them, and got something of value from them. For instance, when *The Old Man and the Sea* was first published in *Life,* September 1, 1952, Ernest wrote the editors: "I'm very excited about *The Old Man and the Sea* and that it is coming out in *Life* so that many people will read it who could not afford to buy it. That makes me much happier than to have a Nobel Prize. To have you guys being so careful and good about it and so thoughtful is better than any kind of prize."

The second award that came to Ernest that year, presented on July 21, his fifty-fifth birthday, was the

Medal of the Order of Carlos Manuel de Cespedes, the highest honor for a foreigner that Cuba could then bestow. Those who attended the presentation said Ernest's pride in this decoration had been genuine and deeply felt.

Upon winning the Nobel Prize for Literature later in the year, Ernest accepted with grace and humility. When the award, itself, was made, however, he was again conspicuous by his absence. The injuries from the plane crashes earlier in the year were still so troublesome that a trip to Sweden had been unthinkable. Another concern that bothered Ernest greatly was the interruption imposed upon his work-in-progress, which, at the time, was going good, according to his own evaluation.

Yet Ernest fulfilled his obligation of writing a speech of acceptance. In its final version, recorded at his home in Cuba, this simple but magnificent speech is made up of only a half dozen paragraphs, totalling scarcely over three hundred words. It was read by John Cabot, the United States Ambassador to Sweden, in the Town Hall at Stockholm on the evening of December 10, 1954.

Despite the pandemonium which had set in from the excitement of newsmen and other intruders at Finca Vigia, the disorientation from his routine of writing, and the continuing acute discomfort in his back, Ernest, characteristically, did not forget his friends. Slightly over a week after the Nobel Prize had been awarded, I received a Christmas card from the Hemingways with a signed note in Ernest's handwriting:

"Am so sorry I have been so bad about writing letters. Everything is clearing up ok although it has been a little bit difficult.

"Have a fine Christmas and New Year and accept all best wishes and love for your loyalty and kindness from

Mary and me."

Nine years later I used two sentences from his Nobel speech as an epigraph for a book of essays on fiction: "Things may not be immediately discernible in what a man writes, and in this sometimes he is fortunate. But eventually they are quite clear and by these and the degree of alchemy that he possesses, he will endure or be forgotten."

When Mary Hemingway gave me permission to quote these sentences (saying "I think Papa would be pleased to have you be the one to reissue them"), she told of the time, September 1944, Ernest had taken her to visit Picasso, who was still living in Paris just after the allied arrival there. The painter had been working all during the German occupation, doing things they knew nothing about.

"And so," Mary added, "I was startled to see those, new to me, various angled faces—you know, three noses and five eyes—and after we left to walk back to the Ritz, I remember saying to Papa that I found the new period odd, and didn't understand it.

" 'Never belittle what you don't understand, my kitten,' Ernest replied. 'If you work at it, you may learn and you may understand better.' "

It is interesting, to say the least, to see that Ernest put the essence of the same thought into .the famous Nobel Prize speech ten years later.

VIII.

Ernest approached the late 1950's in his usual cheerful spirits and in good health, with the exception of the continued after effects of his African plane crashes. His weight still around two hundred pounds, he swam a half to three-fourths mile daily in the pool at Finca Vigia for months after returning from New York in the fall of 1957. Through Christmas and into the new year he kept carefully to his regime, working "awfully hard" every day.

In early January he wrote to express his pleasure over the fact that I had liked his two stories in the anniversary issue of *The Atlantic Monthly*. He went on to say that several "guys" whom he respected had written they liked the stories too, which made him feel good. Ernest then added casually that Orville Prescott did not like them and that seemed good to him too.

I was to discover several months later that Ernest had worked almost uninterrupted since our parting in October. The product of those months was a full-sized "thing" completed in the winter. Shortly afterwards he began something else which grew and grew, engaging him to the point where he had to postpone writing even his oldest friends, near and far. In truth, Ernest tore himself away no farther than the telephone and then only for matters of utmost urgency. By late August he had written over 100,000 words on a novel (according to his own count), saying in a letter he was truly ashamed for having been so remiss in his correspondence.

Just as the winter had been the coldest in Cuba's history, that summer, according to the Hemingway's readings, developed into the hottest, with no drop into coolness at night so that human energies could be recouped and also without the steady east breeze which ordinarily cooled the Finca hilltop. As a consequence, Ernest and Mary anticipated the happy prospect of getting away to somewhere cool in September.

This was the period when someone tried to reprove Ernest for not having attended the funeral of a celebrated acquaintance.

"A son of a bitch alive is a son of a bitch dead," he countered with that quickness of wit for which he was always so remarkable.

In the spring of 1959, Ernest returned to Cuba via Key West from Idaho, where he and Mary had spent the better part of the preceding six months. The trip by automobile gave him a chance to see a fine slice of the country, including Las Vegas, Phoenix, El Paso, Juárez, Eagle Pass, Laredo, Corpus Christi, New Orleans, Panama City, Apalachicola, Sarasota, and Key West. Someone split the driving with Ernest as far as New Orleans but Ernest drove alone from there on to Florida. He saw the second part of Playhouse 90 version of *For Whom the Bell Tolls* in Phoenix and visited his old friend Waldo Peirce in Tucson. His reaction to the television show seemed favorable, with particular compliments to the performance by the young actress who portrayed Maria.

All of his life Ernest was known for his sense of humor, manifest in his tongue-in-cheek conversation and in his inimitable manner of writing. During the years I knew him, his habit of not taking himself too seriously and his ability to laugh at himself were constantly in evidence. Whether these took the form of his pose as Dr. Hemingstein or an occasional parody of his own writing, Ernest managed to smile at himself and others even when the going was toughest. One of my favorite anecdotes showing this side of Ernest was related by Valerie Danby-Smith, who became his secretary in July 1959, and who worked for the Hemingway estate assembling papers to be presented to the John F. Kennedy Memorial Library.

Soon after Miss Danby-Smith was employed as his secretary, they were passing the house where James Joyce had lived in Paris. Ernest recalled how he often brought the Irish novelist home following an evening's drinking, and Nora would open the door and say, "Well, here comes James Joyce the writer, drunk again with Ernest Hemingway." And he chuckled as he told it, imitating Nora's Irish accent.

That spring and summer Ernest covered the bullfights for *Life* magazine. These were to establish Luis Miguel Dominguin or Antonio Ordonez as *El Numero Uno* during the "dangerous summer." Later in the fall Ernest wrote from Malaga, their base, that he was working on an addendum to *Death in the Afternoon,* some of which was to be published in *Life.* For months the Hemingway *cuadrilla* had been on the road like gypsies but without gypsy leisure. According to his judgment, if he could get the piece right, it would give some idea of what they had

57

been doing. "It was a marvelous summer," he stated. "One of the best I've ever had."

Ernest joined Mary in Cuba the first week in November. By the middle of the month they had left for Ketchum, Idaho, where they remained through Christmas and into January. Having shattered her left elbow on November 22, Mary underwent lengthy treatment. First, the doctors put her arm in a cast with the arm straight down; then after three weeks, or thereabouts, rebroke the elbow and put on a new cast with the elbow bent at a ninety-degree angle. After the second cast was removed, therapy was started to loosen up the arm. Ernest took her to the hospital in Sun Valley each morning for an extended period, looked after her, and did the errands. A blizzard set in Christmas Eve, knocking out telephones and electricity. Added to that, temperatures ranged from fifteen to twenty below zero for the following two weeks. During the period surrounding Christmas, Ernest did no writing except to pay bills.

Regardless of these complications he had to be back in Cuba not later than the middle of January in order to finish some urgent work. His plans were to stay on in Cuba until mid-summer. However rough things had been with the Hemingways, there were no outward complaints—only an apology for not having written during Christmas.

For several years I had tried unsuccessfully to find a bronze bust of Ernest, which I could place in my private library. Finally, though, I asked his opinion of the Hemingway head sculptured by Robert Berks and used in a television series featuring some of Ernest's stories. On television the statue seemed authentic and lifelike, although it was known that Berks had made it from

Head of Ernest Hemingway, sculptured by Robert Berks, 1959. (Photo by Robert Berks)

photographs, not from life. Certainly, I did not want to have a duplicate of the original made if Ernest had a low opinon of this work by Berks.

A reply came by letter in April 1960. Ernest's attitude appeared unequivocal—"an ok statue," the original of which a friend was getting for Mary, who liked it. Ernest said he thought it a shame that I should have to buy it, adding that he would be delighted to give me the original Mary was getting but he thought she should probably keep it to excerise her right to heave it at him if the necessity should ever arise. Then he suggested he split the cost with me. Of course, I would not accept his generosity but, knowing he did not dislike the bronze head, I authorized Robert Berks to cast another one for me. This statue was delivered from New York in late May.

Ernest's letter expressed his view that statues of living people tended to "spook" him a little but "due to our own vulnerability you never know when they may come in useful." Kiddingly phrased, his terminal comment on the bronze head was that perhaps we could find a suitable structure to mount it on in the event he should have the belated satisfaction of dying any place except in a self-rumpled bed.

Ernest also reported that he had been working very hard on *The Dangerous Summer,* having something over 70,000 words done on the project. Truly, it had been a quiet, pleasant spring. None of the political turbulence in Cuba seemed to have penetrated Finca Vigia, where the Hemingways worked and swam, ate and drank, and were apparently happy—a situation that continued into that summer.

In July a letter written by Valerie Danby-Smith arrived, thanking me in behalf of "Papa and Mary" for a

Smithfield ham I had recently given them. As a matter of fact, I had made a pleasant habit of sending them several genuine Smithfield hams annually for the past few years—such hams being among the very few things they could not get easily, themselves. Miss Danby-Smith went on to say that "you will be pleased to hear we have enjoyed many a good meal of Virginia ham remembering you in gratitude, and always the same question arises, 'Who has written to Bill Seward to thank him?' I remember what a great event the arrival of the Virginia ham was. It was too large to be cooked on the oven, so a great fire was built outdoors, and all the household would stop by at invervals to check the progress."

Actually, Ernest had been so busy on the "bull piece" that he barely took a day off in every two weeks. And though Mary's arm had improved enormously, it still required a lot of working on, daily massage and exercises. In all the years I knew Ernest, this was his only letter that was not written personally.

It should be noted, also, that Ernest's secretary asserted, referring to the summer 1960, "Things in general are not too good here, but there is no need to tell you about that." Otherwise, there was nothing that could be called news or even gossip.

IX.

As Miss Danby-Smith implied, the disastrous nature of the Castro government had finally become apparent. Not long after her letter arrived around the middle of July, the Hemingways quietly left San Francisco de Paula with numerous pieces of luggage but having every intention to return. Actually, they kept their entire staff of nine at full salary, as they always did, with the house running as usual and their animals cared for. That fall, however, they moved on from New York to Ketchum, Idaho, where they had bought a house. Things began to go badly for Ernest, and rapidly. In November he entered St. Mary's Hospital of the Mayo Clinic under the name of his doctor from Ketchum. Thus until his real identity was discovered by newsmen in January, he was known for a time as George Saviers.

After several weeks he was released but his condition forced him to return in the spring. Finally, he left St. Mary's the last week in June. With a friend he and Mary drove to Ketchum, the arduous trip taking five days. According to some of those who were there, Ernest seemed to be noticeably relieved upon arrival home. Saturday night Ernest and Mary had a quiet dinner at a local inn. Then the next day—that hot, bright Sunday morning in July—one of this century's greatest writers departed from the living.

When news of the "incredible accident" reached me that afternoon in Virginia, small wonder it was that my immediate reaction was one of incomprehension. More than a week passed before I undertook to write Mary. Nevertheless, in that letter I reminded her that I had never known a man who inspired true affection like Ernest did. Among other things, I wrote, "But we will all have to be thankful for knowing him for as long as we did. Happily, he'll remain in his books as long as the language is read."

Indeed, the readability of Ernest's works is much in evidence already, just as it has been since the beginning of his literary career. Now a few years after Ernest's death, Eric Moon, Editor of the *Library Journal* reports that if anyone compiled a list of the "best-read" books, Hemingway's name would have rested securely on top for years. The American Library Association, in fact, has made nation-wide surveys of libraries to find out about reading trends. The first survey instructed librarians to comment upon American reading habits over the previous five years. The results were announced in January 1962. Subsequent releases have been in the form of annual polls. The listings include the most read author. According to Eric Moon, only two names have appeared *every* year since the surveys started, one of the two being Hemingway, who, the first survey commented, was "way out in front," where he has been each year since.

In my opinion, the really outstanding quality of

Ernest Hemingway, the man and the writer, was his soundness. It was no surprise to me, therefore, when his brother, Leicester, concurred in this appraisal, expressing his own view of Ernest in 1965: "He was one amazingly sound guy, in his areas of soundness. And he taught with unconscious ease all of us who sweated and swivited to learn."

This soundness revealed itself in many ways, particularly in his individuality, his horror of pretense, and his love of simplicity. The legend fails to take into account this side of Hemingway. Fond of simple clothes, Ernest wore no jewelry nor did he ever smoke, except Cuban cigarettes for several years when he first began fishing out of Havana. After his death someone asked Mary whether he smoked a pipe.

"No indeed," she replied. "I am sure Papa would have regarded smoking a pipe as being pretentious."

Though he ate moderately, Ernest was a true gourmet and a connoisseur of wine. He liked Chinese food best of all, according to Mary, who learned to cook some twenty Chinese dishes. He also liked many of the Cuban creole dishes, Italian and French food, and all the American classic dishes.

Always a man of "style" (in the best sense of the word), Ernest never did anything because it was supposed to be "sophisticated" or fashionable. In this connection, his absolute refusal to appear on radio, television, and the lecture circuit is well known. Even after it became fashionable in the 1950's for universities to subsidize authors by way of lectureships and as writers-in-residence, Ernest continued to follow his own individual principles and never gave in to pressures. When William Faulkner was at the University of Virginia and many lesser writers set up headquarters at colleges and

63

universities all over the country, Ernest consistently turned down lucrative offers from leading universities, including Yale.

He was not only understandably averse to the academic world but Ernest was convinced that the writer is not a teacher nor a professional speaker, but his one duty is to write. Although his three sons are all college men, Ernest never had any direct affiliation with a specific American college or university nor did he ever express an interest in any single one. As far as I know, his nearest personal approach to an educational institution came when he drove down from Ketchum to Hailey (Ezra Pound's home-town) one night in the very late 1950's and gave an informal talk to the high school students there.

Hemingway's favorite Colt .22 automatic pistol, incased.
Gift from Mary Hemingway to William Seward, 1963.
(Photo by author)

X.

More and more in later years Ernest believed in short books. At least upon one occasion that I am aware of, he expressed the notion that a book should not be so large that it could not be held comfortably while you read lying down. This idea he put into practice, certainly, in *Across the River, The Old Man and the Sea,* and *A Moveable Feast.*

Another conviction that became more entrenched as he grew older found expression in these words, "If anyone gets bored, it's his own damned fault." Come to think of it, it is hard to imagine this man ever having been bored in a lifetime concerned with adventure and death, tenderness and generosity, the humorous and the true. Ernest Hemingway was a happy man and those who knew him will always remember him that way.

Looking back, the reader will observe that I have consistently addressed him as Ernest. It is fairly common knowledge that he disliked his given name, a reaction shared by many people regarding their own names. Yet his oldest and closest friends, including his only brother, called him Ernest, although when they were young, Leicester also called him Stein. The term "Papa" came into the picture rather late.

As a writer Ernest never relied seriously upon journals, for he possessed an uncanny memory and his ability to assimilate and retain details of almost unlimited sorts was amazing, to say the least. These capacities he retained up into the last months of his life, during which time he continued to work on his Paris sketches, that posthumous book that was almost universally commended for its accuracy of detail and for its impeccable style. When *A Moveable Feast* was published in 1964, I wrote a review which appeared in abbreviated form. Because of its pertinency to what I have recorded in these recollections and also because Mary has referred to it as a "comprehending review," I am including the original version here:

A *Moveable Feast* proves beyond any doubt what some of us have known all along—that the real apprenticeship of Ernest Hemingway as a writer of fiction occurred not in the news rooms of Kansas City or Toronto but in Paris during the early 1920's. When he recorded reminiscences of those days, the author chose to write about himself by indirection, or, as he himself called it, by "remate" (I am sure he regarded the autobiography or full memoir of a professional writer as being pretentious and superfluous).

In method the Paris sketches are somewhat akin to the dramatic monologue in which the subject reveals himself by talking about others. Yet Hemingway's book is infinitely more complex than that nineteenth-century poetic form. Here the master technician uses the methods of fiction he perfected during a lifetime in order to write about actual people, places, and happenings. Indeed, *A Moveable Feast* would be an important book if it did nothing beyond proving that the portrayal of the shape of a place in actuality and the pattern of factual action over a

Guests at the Annual Dinner of the Poetry Society of
America, Astor Hotel, New York City, January 1963.
(Photo courtesy of Poetry Society of America)

duration of time, when truly presented, can compete with a "work of the imagination."

Completed not many months before his death in 1961, the book indicates, futhermore, that the artist was in full control of his creative facilities over the whole distance, for the writing itself is vintage Hemingway.

Scores have recorded their versions of Paris in the 1920's but no one has written as well as Hemingway about spring in that romantic city. None of the others possessed the acute consciousness of sensation that was his nor has any been able to pin down with words quite so clearly and impressively the atmosphere or "feel"; the cafés, including descriptions of innumerable foods and drinks, the favorite streets on the Left Bank, the Rue de Seine, the Boulevard St.-Michel, the Rue Bonaparte, St.-Germain des Prés—the Grande Boulevards which flourished with gay stalls showing clothing, candy, and trinkets for sale. Paris, of course, is not the Eiffel Tower and the Arch of Triumph.

These, then, are sketches of places, of people, of work, of play, of happiness, and of hunger. Most of all, the book conveys Hemingway's consciousness of the impact of Paris upon the young apprentice-artist: "If you are lucky enough to have lived in Paris as a young man, then wherever you go for the rest of your life, it stays with you, for Paris is a moveable feast."

The portraits of his friends and acquaintances (Pound, Stein, Ford, Lewis, Fitzgerald, to mention a few) make abundantly clear Hemingway's hatred of stupidity, disloyalty, and self-aggrandizement while, at the same time, they reveal his passionate love and respect for honesty, fidelity, and moral strength. These traits remained with him throughout life. The "refracted" portrait of himself is paradoxical, to be sure, picturing the evolution of a genius who had an amazing capacity for friendship and whose generosity and tolerance, even after all the intervening years, permitted him to be extremely kind to Scott Fitzgerald in the longest single sketch.

I should think it highly improbable that any future

67

biographer will be able to catch on the printed page that ambivalence which was peculiarly Hemingway's; yet it comes through in his sketches and literally bounces off almost every page of the book. Actually, it seems incredible that any man could look back over thirty years and then write of specifics with such accuracy and precision. Here Hemingway records sensations and moods as freshly and enthusiastically as he did in those marvelous early stories and in *The Sun Also Rises* in 1926. A typical pastoral fragment reads:

"With so many trees in the city, you could see the spring coming each day until a night of warm wind would bring it suddenly in one morning. Sometimes the heavy cold rains would beat it back so that it would seem that it would never come and that you were losing a season out of your life. This was the only truly sad time in Paris because it was unnatural. You expected to be sad in the fall. Part of you died each year when the leaves fell from the trees and their branches were bare against the wind and the cold, wintry light. But you knew there would always be the spring, as you knew the river would flow again after it was frozen. When the cold rains kept on and killed the spring, it was as though a young person had died for no reason."

All of these things notwithstanding, there will be a handful of the fraternity of pedants, I am sure, whose frustration over Hemingway's own private spelling, which includes as extra "e" in the title, will prevent them from approaching the book calmly—a situation that would be of no concern to Hemingway, for while he was alive, the opinions of these people seldom entered into his thinking.

Reviewing one of his novels some years ago, I made the statement that publication of a new book by Hemingway is always a literary event. Considering the impact of his death upon the publishing world and in view of the general state of current writing in the United States, I venture to suggest that this observation is even more applicable to a posthumous book of his.

Mary Hemingway fishing on Chesapeake Bay, May 1963.
(Photo by author)

XI.

It takes a strong man to survive his own fame. This Ernest did for thirty-five years. Even toward the end when things began to go so badly, courage never deserted him. What finally failed him was his body. As Leicester Hemingway has said, "This can happen to anyone." All along Ernest was so intensely aware of the role of violence in human existence and what the ever-present consciousness of death can do to man that only the simple desires seemed to count as against any traditionally conceived values except those of honesty towards oneself and of loyalty to others.

Ernest was one of the best of human beings, a fact that anyone who knew him sensed. And so, like authentic heroes of other days, he lives on in the minds of the living, which is probably the greatest contribution any man can make to the members of the human race.

XI.